SMALL ANIMALS

MICHAEL CHINERY
ILLUSTRATED BY IAN JACKSON

Kingfisher Books

Advisers: Mary Jane Drummond,
Tutor in Primary Education,
Cambridge Institute of Education, Cambridge
Iris Walkinshaw, Headteacher, Rushmore Infants
School, Hackney, London

Kingfisher Books, Grisewood & Dempsey Ltd
Elsley House, 24–30 Great Titchfield Street,
London W1P 7AD

First published in 1988 by Kingfisher Books

BRITISH CATALOGUING IN PUBLICATION DATA
Chinery, Michael
Small animals.—(Stepping stones 4, 5, 6).
1. Animals—Juvenile literature
I. Title   II. Jackson, Ian, *1960*— III. Series
591   QL49
ISBN: 0 86272 337 X

Edited by Vanessa Clarke
Editorial assistant: Camilla Hallinan
Designed by Ben White
Cover designed by Pinpoint Design Company
Phototypeset by Southern Positives and Negatives
(SPAN), Lingfield, Surrey
Colour separations by Newsele Litho Ltd, Milan
Printed in Spain

Contents

4

Thousands of animals live in and around your home but you will have to look very carefully to find them.

In this garden it does not look as if there are any animals. But there are hundreds. They are difficult to see because they are so small. And most of them are hiding because it is daytime.

The animals in this book are all smaller than this house mouse.

Small animals are hunted by birds and other larger animals. Many of them would be eaten if they did not hide, so during the day we·have to look hard for them.

Try looking for them yourself in the summer. You can see them more clearly if you use a magnifying glass.

These three different animals lay their eggs in houses. Carpet beetles lay their eggs under woollen carpets. The larvae which hatch from the eggs eat the carpet wool. When they are fully grown the larvae change into beetles. The beetles fly outside.

Clothes moths lay their eggs in woollen clothes and blankets because their larvae feed on wool too. The adult moths do not eat at all.

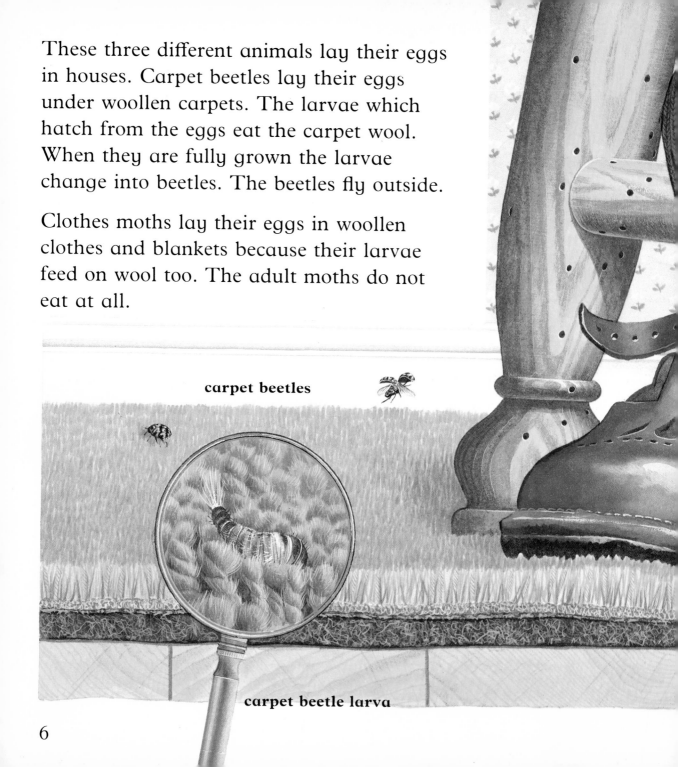

carpet beetles

carpet beetle larva

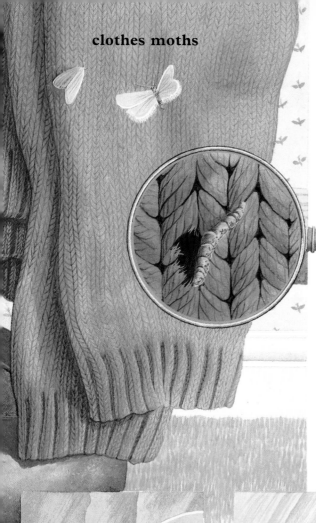

clothes moths

clothes moth larva

The woodworm is the larva of a small brown beetle called a furniture beetle. The beetle lays its eggs in tiny cracks in furniture and other wood including dead trees.

When the larvae hatch out of the eggs, they chew tunnels through the wood. They live in the tunnels until they turn into beetles. The adult beetles chew neat little holes to get out of the wood and fly away.

woodworm eggs

woodworm larva

furniture beetle

bluebottle's foot

You often hear flies even when you can't see them. But flies do not have voices. The buzzing noise is made by their wings moving up and down.

These flies are bluebottles. They are also called blowflies. They can walk on ceilings, walls and windows because they have tiny claws and suction pads on their feet.

8

This bluebottle has come into the house to look for food. When it finds some food, it dribbles saliva over it to make it liquid. Then it mops up the liquid with a spongy pad around its mouth. The saliva leaves little brown stains.

bluebottle feeding

Centipedes and woodlice like damp dark places outside the house. They hide during the day because they don't like dry air and light.

This centipede has thirty legs but some have more than a hundred legs. Centipedes leave their hiding places at night and hunt other small animals.

centipede catching a moth

Woodlice trundle about at night. They nibble the plants that grow on stones and tree trunks. You can find them easily under flowerpots and stones and in tiny cracks in walls during the day. But remember to put them back where you found them because woodlice die quickly in dry air.

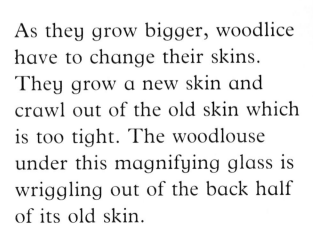

As they grow bigger, woodlice have to change their skins. They grow a new skin and crawl out of the old skin which is too tight. The woodlouse under this magnifying glass is wriggling out of the back half of its old skin.

11

Ants live together in big nests called colonies, which they build under paths and large stones. In each nest there is one large female who lays all the eggs. She is called the queen. The other ants are called workers. They build the nest, keep it clean, collect food, and look after the queen and her eggs and larvae.

nursery

larvae

eggs

queen

When the workers find some greenfly, they milk them like cows. They do this to get the sweet honeydew that the greenfly make in their bodies.

The ant nest has lots of rooms called chambers. The upper ones are the nurseries where the larvae live. If you disturb a nest the workers hurry to the nurseries and carry the larvae to a safe place lower down in the nest.

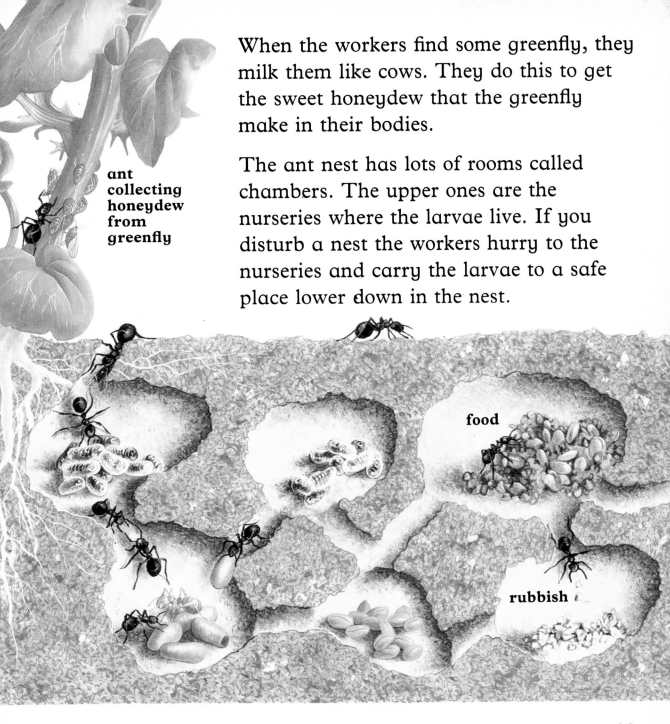

ant collecting honeydew from greenfly

food

rubbish

Earthworms live under the ground where there is soft damp soil. They make tunnels by swallowing mouthfuls of soil. Then they digest the tiny bits of dead plants in the soil. The rest of the soil passes right through their bodies and ends up in little heaps on top of the ground. These are called wormcasts.

You can feel a worm's tiny bristles if you stroke it gently.

On warm damp nights worms often search for food above the ground. They keep their tail ends in their burrows. Then they drag dead leaves into their tunnels to eat later. Tiny bristles on their undersides help worms to grip the soil so they can shoot back underground if they are disturbed. But sometimes a thrush is too quick for them.

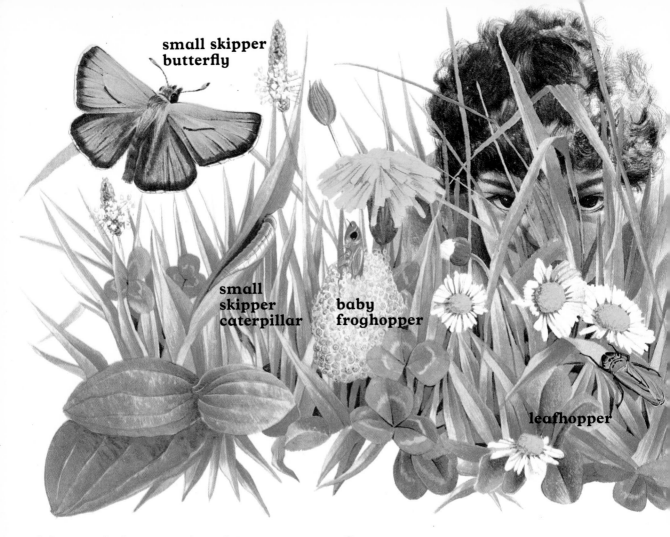

small skipper
butterfly

small
skipper
caterpillar

baby
froghopper

leafhopper

Most of these animals use camouflage to stop
other animals from finding and eating them.
The caterpillar of the small skipper butterfly
rolls a leaf into a tube and hides inside it.
Young froghopper bugs make blobs of froth to
hide in. The froth is often called cuckoospit,
but it has nothing to do with cuckoos at all.

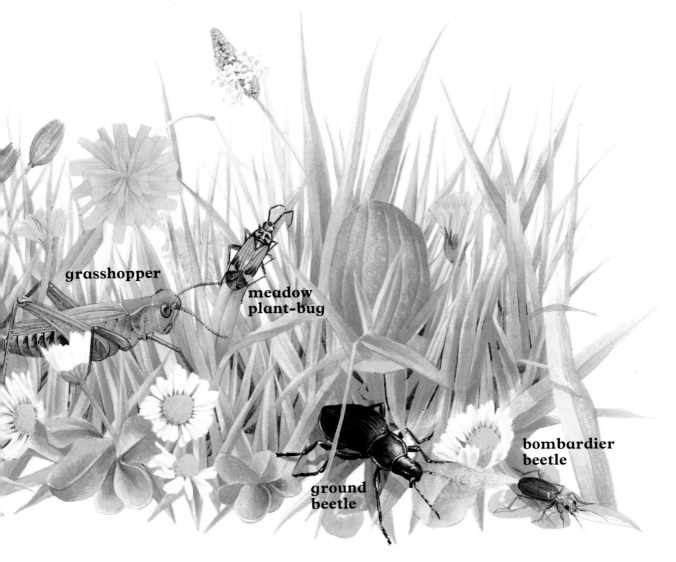

grasshopper

meadow
plant-bug

ground
beetle

bombardier
beetle

The leafhopper and the grasshopper are hard to
see because they are green like the grass. The
meadow plant-bug is easy to see, but birds know
that it has a nasty taste and they leave it alone.
The bombardier beetle does not need camouflage.
It defends itself by squirting poisonous gases.

These honeybees are collecting nectar and pollen from flowers. They suck up the nectar to take back to the hive where they live, and they carry the pollen on their hind legs. Thousands of honeybees live in a hive which contains thousands of wax cells. There is one queen bee. Most of the bees are workers.

Worker bees make the cells out of wax from their bodies. They store pollen in some cells. They turn nectar into honey and store it in other cells.

The queen lays an egg in each empty cell and tiny larvae hatch out in about three days. Workers feed them with honey and pollen for about nine days. Then the larvae are fully grown and workers cover the cells with wax. The larvae turn into new bees about ten days later.

The youngest workers keep the nest clean, but as they get older they start to feed the next batch of larvae. Later on they become builders. Only the oldest workers go out to collect nectar and pollen.

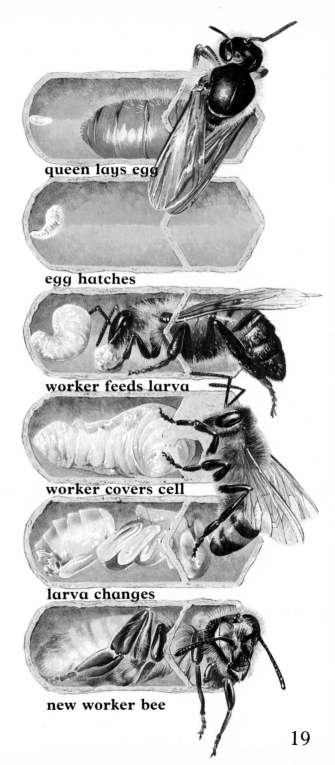

queen lays egg

egg hatches

worker feeds larva

worker covers cell

larva changes

new worker bee

19

This is a red admiral butterfly. It uses its tongue like a tiny straw to suck nectar from flowers. When the butterfly is not feeding it keeps its tongue curled up under its head.

The female red admiral lays her eggs on stinging nettles. A spiky caterpillar hatches from each egg. It rolls up leaves to make a little tent and feeds inside it. When it is fully grown the caterpillar hangs upside-down and turns into a chrysalis. The butterfly is formed inside the chrysalis. When it is ready it breaks out and flies away.

butterfly

laying egg

egg hatching

caterpillar making a tent

chrysalis

breaking out of chrysalis

caterpillar feeding

21

Ladybirds are the gardener's friends because they eat the greenfly which damage plants. Their larvae eat greenfly too. Different kinds of ladybirds have different numbers of spots, but they all have two pairs of wings. The spotty part of the ladybird is the front pair of wings. The back pair of wings is folded up underneath. You see both pairs only when a ladybird is flying.

snail feeding

snail laying eggs

baby snails

Snails usually curl up inside their shells in the daytime. They look for food at night. Snails lay soft round eggs. Tiny snails hatch from them. Unlike baby ladybirds, baby snails look just like their parents.

laying
eggs

ladybird
eating
greenfly

pupa

eggs
hatching

young
ladybird

larva eating
greenfly

23

This garden spider makes a web shaped like a wheel to trap flies and other insects. The web is made of very fine threads of silk which the spider pulls from the back of its body. The circular threads are coated with glue to trap the insects. The spider does not get trapped because it walks only on the spokes of the web and these are not sticky.

spinning a life-line

wrapping eggs

spiderlings hatch

If spiders fall they spin silken life-lines to save themselves. Female spiders wrap their eggs in silk. Baby spiders use tiny threads of silk as parachutes to float away to other parts of the garden.

wasp feeding

Wasps live in large colonies. Each colony has a queen. In the early summer wasps are busy collecting caterpillars and other small animals to feed the thousands of larvae in the nest. By the end of the summer these larvae have all grown up and the wasps have no more work to do. They spend their time munching fruit and other sweet things. In the autumn nearly all the wasps die.

Earwigs like fruit too and often nestle in the hollows around the stalks of apples in the daytime. They come out to feed at night.

If you pick up an earwig it will wave its pincers at you. It is trying to frighten you but it cannot hurt you.

Earwigs wave their pincers to frighten off other animals.

Lots of the small animals we have read about come out of their hiding places at night when the air is cooler and damper. Centipedes and woodlice climb walls and tree trunks to look for food. Earwigs feed on flower petals and snails browse on tiny plants. Snails leave silvery trails of slime which show you where they have been.

Most birds sleep at night but small animals still have to watch out for other hunting animals. Hedgehogs and mice search for slugs and beetles, and bats swoop through the air to catch moths.

Bluebottles and most other flies settle down to sleep when it gets dark, but this is when the daddy-long-legs wakes up. It often comes through the window and then buzzes noisily as it tries to get out again. Some people are frightened of daddy-long-legs, but they cannot hurt you.

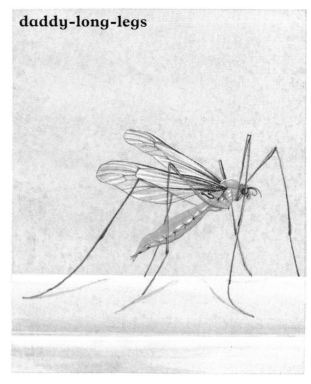
daddy-long-legs

house spider

Long-legged house spiders often fall into the bath at night while looking for places to hang their webs. They need help to get out again because they cannot climb up the steep sides. House spiders cannot hurt you. But some mosquitoes bite. Sometimes at night you can hear the whine of their

mosquito feeding

wings. Male mosquitoes feed on nectar but female mosquitoes feed on blood. They have mouths like injection needles which they stick into skin.

Listen hard and you may hear other noises. A house is full of sounds at night. Perhaps a mouse will scamper through the roof or under the floorboards. Even if you cannot see them, small animals are all around you.

Index